Do We Have Immortal Souls

Bible Studies, Volume 6

Leslie Rendell

Published by Leslie Rendell, 2023.

Table of Contents

Why should we study the bible? Isn't it enough to go to church once a week and listen to the Pastor?

Most Pastors who belong to one of the modern day churches have to follow what the church leaders tell them. They all have their own "statement of beliefs" to adhere too, and these doctrines vary from church to church in what they see as the truth. So since they cannot all be right, then some must be wrong. What if that refers to the church you are attending, if indeed you attend any church at all? How can you know what God sees as the truth? Well, it is up to the individual to sort the wheat from the chaff. How do we do that? Only by seeking the truth that God has concealed in his book, the bible.

Consider the following passage of scripture in the book of Proverbs.

> *Pro 25:2 It is the glory of God to conceal things, but the glory of kings is to search things out.*

This is what God expects from us. We are to look into the holy scriptures constantly and find the truth that he has concealed there for us to uncover. Please notice that God has not concealed them from us to keep it all a secret. No, he wants us to look for the truth. This is further emphasized in the following verses from the book of Isaiah:

> *Isa 28:9 "To whom will he teach knowledge, and to whom will he explain the message? Those who are weaned from the milk, those taken from the breast?"*

> *Isa 28:10 For it is precept upon precept, precept upon precept, line upon line, line upon line, here a little, there a little.*

This backs up what we read in Proverbs 25:2: that we must search out a matter that God has concealed. This is a real treasure hunt. If we can seek the will of God in our lives, we are not rejecting him, but we are embracing him and his way of life. There is a glorious reward for those who are prepared to seek God with their whole hearts. Read the following verse and see what this reward is.

> *Rom 2:7 To those who by persistence in doing good seek glory, honor and immortality, he will give eternal life.*

Therefore, we must spend time in searching the scriptures. Looking for precept upon precept, line upon line, here a little, there a little. Looking for the things God has concealed. We must search for these pearls of wisdom God has concealed in his bible.

Chapter 1 - Introduction

Have you ever wondered where the idea of an immortal soul comes from, and if it is correct? It may come as a surprise to you to know that this idea is not found anywhere in the bible.

We all know that death is a reality in this present world. We all live and then one day we all die. There is no escaping this. The very thought of dying is not a very pleasant one, and it is always devastating for those who are left behind. The hope of all people is that the deceased person is still alive in some form and has gone to a better place.

The most common belief among Christians is it that the good go to an eternal reward in a place called Heaven. While those who have done evil during their lives here on the earth are all doomed to go to a place of eternal punishment, usually called Hell.

These beliefs are all based on the idea that all humans have an immortal soul that can never die. But will continue to live on in one or the other of these places. Since the soul is still living after death, then it has to go somewhere. Either to eternal happiness in Heaven, or to eternal torment in Hell. This appears to be the most widely held belief in Christianity.

The truth about humans having an immortal soul differs completely from the above scenario. To fully understand this, we need to go to the word of God, or his holy bible for the correct answer. We need to know why, and how we were created, and why we must all die.

The good news, or the gospel, is that there are rewards for both the good and the evil, but it is not what is commonly taught in traditional churches. The bible will teach us we do not have an immortal soul, and we do not go to either Heaven or Hell when our earthly bodies die. When you understand the truth, it is so much better than what you may hope for. But only if you are prepared to believe the word of God.

Chapter 2 - Do We Have Immortal Souls?

The belief that we all have an immortal soul is widely held by many Christians today. What we must decide is whether this is a man-made idea, or is it actually something that the bible reveals to us? Before we can answer this question, the first thing we must do is to get a definition of the word Immortal.

1. not mortal; not liable or subject to death; undying: our immortal souls.

2. remembered or celebrated through all time.

3. not liable to perish or decay; imperishable; everlasting.

4. perpetual; lasting; constant.

OK, so if we have an immortal soul, this means it can never die. The soul will live on somewhere for all eternity and that will be Heaven or Hell. Depending on how good or bad you were during our lifetime on earth. This is the teaching of the major Christian denominations today.

This idea of immortality of the soul was further influenced by the early Greek philosophers Socrates, Augustine and especially Plato. They all reasoned the soul was separate from the body and would live eternally.

Let us go back to the first book in the Bible. Back to Genesis 2:7 to see how God created the first human, Adam.

> *Gen 2:7 And the LORD God formed man of the dust of the ground, and breathed into his nostrils the breath of life; and man became a living soul.*

The most important thing we must consider here it the fact that when God breathed into Adam's nostrils, he became a living soul. God did not put an immortal soul into Adam when he created him. No, he became a living soul (Nephesh in the Hebrew language) We are all living souls.

So Adam was formed out of the dust of the ground and became a living soul. There is nowhere recorded here that he was then given an immortal soul, just that he became a living soul, a living creature. Therefore, Adam was created as a mortal being, capable of dying and returning to the dust he was created from. Then God created Eve from one of Adam's ribs (yes, I believe this actually happened) Later; they were both guilty of sinning against God by eating from the forbidden fruit in the middle of the garden.

It did not take Satan too long to persuade Adam and Eve to eat of this tree. The tree of the knowledge of good and evil in the middle of the garden. He did this by convincing them they would not die if they ate from this tree as

> *Gen 3:4 The serpent said to the woman, "You won't really die,"*

> *Gen 3:5 for God knows that in the day you eat it, your eyes will be opened, and you will be like God, knowing good and evil.*

In verse four, Satan tells Eve she will not die, and in verse five, she will be like God Himself. Satan used Eve's free will to make the wrong decision. Eve believed Satan's lie that she would not die and that she would be like God and live forever. She could make her own decisions based on what she thought was right or wrong. She no longer wanted God's direction in her life.

We can see the penalty God applied to them for disobeying Him in Gen 3:17-24.

> *Gen 3:17 To Adam he said, "Because you listened to your wife and ate fruit from the tree about which I commanded you, 'You*

must not eat from it,' "Cursed is the ground because of you; through painful toil you will eat food from it all the days of your life.

Gen 3:18 It will produce thorns and thistles for you, and you will eat the plants of the field.

Gen 3:19 By the sweat of your brow you will eat your food until you return to the ground, since from it you were taken; for dust you are and to dust you will return."

Gen 3:20 Adam named his wife Eve, because she would become the mother of all the living.

Gen 3:21 The LORD God made garments of skin for Adam and his wife and clothed them.

Gen 3:22 And the LORD God said, "The man has now become like one of us, knowing good and evil. He must not be allowed to reach out his hand and take also from the tree of life and eat, and live forever."

Gen 3:23 So the LORD God banished him from the Garden of Eden to work the ground from which he had been taken.

Gen 3:24 After he drove the man out, he placed on the east side of the Garden of Eden cherubim and a flaming sword flashing back and forth to guard the way to the tree of life.

Because they sinned, the ground produced thorns and thistles and they were cast out of the garden. God then sets cherubim and a flaming sword to protect the way to the tree of life. He did this to prevent Adam and Eve from returning to the Garden and eating from its fruit. Because if they ate from this tree, they would live forever, they would become immortal. They would live forever in a body that would always be subject to sins and evil. This would be the way they must live for all time. But God prevented them from returning to the garden and eating from the tree of life. Therefore, all mankind will remain mortal beings until Jesus Christ comes to reveal the possibility of immortality.

But before we go there, let us read the following passages of scripture from the old testament. These are referring to all the people who have died and have returned to the dust from which they were created.

> *Psa 6:5 Among the dead no one proclaims your name. Who praises you from the grave?*

> *Ecc 9:5 For the living know that they will die, but the dead know nothing; they have no further reward, and even their name is forgotten.*

> *Ecc 9:10 Whatever your hand finds to do, do it with all your might, for in the realm of the dead, where you are going, there is neither working nor planning nor knowledge nor wisdom.*

And to emphasize this point, we are told we are just the same as other animals. We all have the same breath God breathed into our nostrils to give us life. See this in.

> *Ecc 3:19 Surely the fate of human beings is like that of the animals; the same fate awaits them both: As one dies, so dies the other. All have the same breath; humans have no advantage over animals. Everything is meaningless.*

The same breath God breathed into Adam, he breathed into all animals to give us all life. Not one breath for man and another for the animals. No, we all have the same breath of life.

In the book of 1Kings and between chapters fifteen and twenty-four, there are many instances where someone has died. The bible records their death as "they slept with their fathers". This is a common way the bible describes the death of Kings.

From the old testament, we are not told anywhere we have an immortal soul. We were created mortal because we are not meant to live in these bodies forever, that are subject to sin and corruption. We are instead meant to understand death as a time of sleeping with our fathers. And as we saw in Ecclesiastes 9:5 above, the dead know nothing. They are just asleep so deeply they have no awareness of any kind. And just like we wake up from sleep, we will also one day wake up from death. When Jesus Christ calls us from the grave in the resurrection of the dead when he returns.

Now let us look to the new testament where we are clearly told that God alone is immortal. We mere humans are not immortal and do not have an immortal soul. We are not meant to live forever in our sinful human form. This is revealed to us in 1Ti 6:14-16.

> *1Ti 6:14 to keep this command without spot or blame until the appearing of our Lord Jesus Christ,*
>
> *1Ti 6:15 which God will bring about in his own time—God, the blessed and only Ruler, the King of kings and Lord of lords,*
>
> *1Ti 6:16 who alone is immortal and who lives in unapproachable light, whom no one has seen or can see. To him be honor and might forever. Amen.*

What can be more obvious from these verses than the fact Jesus Christ alone in immortal? Surely, this means that we are not immortal? This is where we must decide whether to believe the teachings of man, or believe the words of God that he has revealed to us in his bible. This false teaching of man having an immortal soul is just one example of the word of God being corrupted. Just to suit the false preachers who want to use the word of God to further their own cause.

We must understand immortality of the soul could only be achieved when Jesus came to the earth. He has bought life and immortality for those who believe in Him. Through his life, death and resurrection, he has made the way possible for mankind to receive immortality, as we see in 2Ti 1:10.

> *2Ti 1:10 but has now been revealed by the appearing of our Savior, Christ Jesus, who abolished death, and brought life and immortality to light through the Good News.*

We may not be born with an immortal soul, but we have been promised by God that a righteous person will surely live. See Eze 18:5-9..

> *Eze 18:5 "But if a man is just, and does that which is lawful and right,*

> *Eze 18:6 and has not eaten on the mountains, hasn't lifted up his eyes to the idols of the house of Israel, hasn't defiled his neighbor's wife, hasn't come near a woman in her impurity,*

> *Eze 18:7 and has not wronged any, but has restored to the debtor his pledge, has taken nothing by robbery, has given his bread to the hungry, and has covered the naked with a garment;*

> *Eze 18:8 he who hasn't lent to them with interest, hasn't taken any increase from them, who has withdrawn his hand from iniquity, has executed true justice between man and man,*

Eze 18:9 has walked in my statutes, and has kept my ordinances, to deal truly; he is just, he shall surely live," says the Lord Yahweh.

But notice what he says in the previous verse.

Eze 18:4 Behold, all souls are mine; as the soul of the father, so also the soul of the son is mine. The soul who sins, he shall die.

The soul who sins, he shall die. If the soul is immortal, then it cannot die. Is there other proof against the immortal soul theory? Look at the following verse.

Mat 10:28 Don't be afraid of those who kill the body, but are not able to kill the soul. Rather, fear him who is able to destroy both soul and body in Gehenna.

Here the author of this book is clearly telling us God can kill both the body and the soul in Gehenna, or Hell. Therefore, the soul can die. It is not immortal.

The word immortality is used only four times in the entire new testament (World English Bible), as listed below.

1Ti 6:15 which in its own times he will show, who is the blessed and only Ruler, the King of kings, and Lord of lords;

1Ti 6:16 who alone has immortality, dwelling in unapproachable light; whom no man has seen, nor can see: to whom be honor and eternal power. Amen.

Who are these verses referring to? It can only be God Himself and here we are told he alone has immortality. Then, in the following verses, we are told we must put on immortality. Something we do not need to do if we already have an immortal soul.

> *1Co 15:53 For this perishable body must become imperishable, and this mortal must put on immortality.*

> *1Co 15:54 But when this perishable body will have become imperishable, and this mortal will have put on immortality, then what is written will happen: "Death is swallowed up in victory."*

These examples from the new testament tell us the thoughts and teachings of an immortal soul are simply incorrect. Immortality belongs only to God, and if mankind wants to be immortal as well, then they must "put it on".

Now look at 2Ti 1:10 and see how Jesus bought immortality to light through the gospel.

> *2Ti 1:10 but it has now been revealed through the appearing of our Savior, Christ Jesus, who has destroyed death and has brought life and immortality to light through the gospel.*

The writer of Proverbs also mentions immortality this way. Along the path of righteousness, we find immortality. So, even in the old testament there are clues to the fact we do not have immortal souls. Once again, we see it is something we must seek and find. To get it, we must travel along the right path, and that simply means we are to live a righteous life.

> *Pro 12:28 In the way of righteousness there is life; along that path is immortality.*

As I have stated before in this book. Now is the time to decide who you are going to believe in this matter that is so vital to your salvation.

The word of God that is contained in his bible, or the false theology that most people accept as the truth. This bible is an incredible book that requires constant study to find all the treasures of truth that it accommodates. The greatest mistake most Christians make today is to just believe what they are told the bible says, without checking the facts for themselves. They are too busy to check. We all understand things differently. Therefore, it is important we do our own research, and especially on matters so vital for us to know.

Another aspect of this to understand is there is no difference between immortality and eternal life. They both mean the same thing. People who have these traits will live on forever. They will never die, or as the book of Revelation puts it. The second death has no power over them. Now let us look at some examples of eternal life to see if they compare with the idea of immortality. As you read, please realise you must get eternal life just the same way you will have to receive immortality. They simply mean the same thing.

When I search for the words "eternal life" in the new testament, I find forty-five references to these words. These verses always explain to us we must receive or inherit eternal life by believing Jesus Christ, and by knowing the only true God. Read the following verses that refer to the time Jesus was in the garden of Gethsemane just prior to his arrest, trial and execution on the Roman cross. Jesus praying to our Heavenly Father says he will give eternal life (immortality) to all those who belong to Him.

> *Joh 17:1 Jesus said these things, and lifting up his eyes to heaven, he said, "Father, the time has come. Glorify your Son, that your Son may also glorify you;*

> *Joh 17:2 even as you gave him authority over all flesh, so he will give eternal life to all whom you have given him.*

I hope you can see a marked difference in what you may have always believed to what the bible actually teaches. There are some forty-five references to eternal life in the new testament. I will add just a few more here to really emphasize the truth. Please read them carefully and look for the clues about how we are to receive eternal life, or immortality.

Mat 19:16 Just then a man came up to Jesus and asked, "Teacher, what good thing must I do to get eternal life?"

Mat 19:29 And everyone who has left houses or brothers or sisters or father or mother or wife or children or fields for my sake will receive a hundred times as much and will inherit eternal life.

Mat 25:46 "Then they will go away to eternal punishment, but the righteous to eternal life."

Joh 3:36 Whoever believes in the Son has eternal life, but whoever rejects the Son will not see life, for God's wrath remains on them.

Joh_5:24 "Very truly I tell you, whoever hears my word and believes him who sent me has eternal life and will not be judged but has crossed over from death to life."

Joh 6:39 This is the will of my Father who sent me, that of all he has given to me I should lose nothing, but should raise him up at the last day.

Joh 6:40 This is the will of the one who sent me, that everyone who sees the Son, and believes in him, should have eternal life; and I will raise him up at the last day."

I sincerely hope you will believe what you have just read in the preceding verses. Remember, there are a lot more in the new testament if you will search for them. And this should be proof positive we are not born with an immortal soul. Immortal means to never die. Eternal life has the same meaning.

Now consider one of the best and most repeated verses in the entire bible. John 3:16.

> *Joh 3:16 For God so loved the world, that he gave his one and only Son, that whoever believes in him should not perish, but have eternal life.*

Notice that it is whoever believes in Him (in Jesus Christ) they shall not perish but will have eternal life. They will inherit immortality. Those who do not believe in Him will not have immortality.

In his letter to Titus, Paul spoke of his hope in eternal life that was promised from God since even before the creation.

> *Tit 1:1 Paul, a servant of God, and an apostle of Jesus Christ, according to the faith of God's chosen ones, and the knowledge of the truth which is according to godliness,*

> *Tit 1:2 in hope of eternal life, which God, who can't lie, promised before time began;*

Through the good news, the gospel of Jesus Christ, he has made it possible for us to have eternal life, to become immortal. So, how did he do this for us? The answer is in the following 2 verses.

> *Joh 6:51 I am the living bread which came down out of heaven. If anyone eats of this bread, he will live forever. Yes, the bread which I will give for the life of the world is my flesh.*

Joh 6:58 This is the bread which came down out of heaven—not as our fathers ate the manna, and died. He who eats this bread will live forever.

Exactly what did Jesus Christ mean by eating his flesh and drinking his blood? He is obviously not talking about cannibalism. No, he means that eating his flesh and drinking his blood is another way of saying we must take in all that Jesus represents. We must believe in Him, as we see in Joh 6:47-51.

Joh 6:47 Most certainly, I tell you, he who believes in me has eternal life.

Joh 6:48 I am the bread of life.

Joh 6:49 Your fathers ate the manna in the wilderness, and they died.

Joh 6:50 This is the bread which comes down out of heaven, that anyone may eat of it and not die.

Joh 6:51 I am the living bread which came down out of heaven. If anyone eats of this bread, he will live forever. Yes, the bread which I will give for the life of the world is my flesh."

In verse 47, Jesus explains it is the one who believes in Him that has eternal life. Then later in the book of John, Jesus warns them not to work for food that will spoil. But to work for food that leads to eternal life. The crowd, not understanding, then asked Jesus what works they must do, and Jesus responds in verse 29. "The work of God is this: to believe in the one he has sent." Jesus is not asking us to be cannibals. He is asking us to just believe in Him, or to do the works he has given each one of us to do, as is written for us in Joh 6:27-29.

Joh 6:27 Don't work for the food which perishes, but for the food which remains to eternal life, which the Son of Man will give to you. For God the Father has sealed him."

Joh 6:28 They said therefore to him, "What must we do, that we may work the works of God?"

Joh 6:29 Jesus answered them, "This is the work of God, that you believe in him whom he has sent."

This idea of believing in Jesus is reinforced in Joh 6:40.

Joh 6:40 "For my Father's will is that everyone who looks to the Son and believes in him shall have eternal life, and I will raise them up at the last day."

Therefore, to eat the flesh and drink the blood of Jesus simply means to believe in Him. To follow Him, and accept Him as our Lord of lords and King of kings. If we do this, an amazing thing will happen. Jesus will raise them up from the dead on the last day. Or as 1Cor 15:53-54 describes.

1Co 15:53 For this perishable body must become imperishable, and this mortal must put on immortality.

1Co 15:54 But when this perishable body will have become imperishable, and this mortal will have put on immortality, then what is written will happen: "Death is swallowed up in victory."

Do you see the significance of these verses? We must put on immortality. We do not need to put on something we already have. No, immortality is something we must search for or to seek, as we see in the following verse of Rom 2:6-8.

Rom 2:6 who "will pay back to everyone according to their works:"

Rom 2:7 to those who by perseverance in well-doing seek for glory, honor, and incorruptibility, eternal life;

Rom 2:8 but to those who are self-seeking, and don't obey the truth, but obey unrighteousness, will be wrath and indignation,

Another passage of scripture from the old testament is Mal 4:2-3. Here the wicked are described as ashes under the soles of the feet of the righteous. They have been completely burned up. There is nothing left of them except ashes. And no immortal soul to carry on living for all eternity.

Mal 4:2 But to you who fear my name shall the sun of righteousness arise with healing in its wings. You will go out, and leap like calves of the stall.

Mal 4:3 You shall tread down the wicked; for they will be ashes under the soles of your feet in the day that I make," says Yahweh of Armies.

And what does 1Cr 15:54 mean, death has been swallowed up in victory? The answer to this is found in Rev 21:3-4.

Rev 21:3 I heard a loud voice out of heaven saying, "Behold, God's dwelling is with people, and he will dwell with them, and they will be his people, and God himself will be with them as their God.

Rev 21:4 He will wipe away every tear from their eyes. Death will be no more; neither will there be mourning, nor crying, nor pain, any more. The first things have passed away."

Verse 3 tells us God will dwell with his people. We will see him as he is. Then in verse 4, we have this amazing promise from God: there will be no more death, mourning, crying or pain.

Please understand what we read here. We must put on immortality because we do not already have it. Our perishable bodies, made from the dust of the ground, must become imperishable, or immortal. Notice we are told we must put on immortality. Something we would not need to do if we already had an immortal soul. If God can destroy both the body and the soul, then we are not immortal, as we can see in Mat 10:28.

Mat 10:28 Do not be afraid of those who kill the body but cannot kill the soul. Rather, be afraid of the One who can destroy both soul and body in hell.

So what can we learn from all this? First, we are created from dust and are not born immortal because God alone is immortal. Jesus came to earth born of a woman and when he was crucified, he took our sins away and gave us all the chance to have eternal life. And the way we have this amazing gift of eternal life is by believing Jesus is the Son of God.

This may sound simple, but it will require us to make some enormous changes to the way we live. This will cause a lot of opposition from family and friends, something we must expect, but resist, and remain loyal to Jesus regardless of the price we must pay. The rewards will far outweigh any troubles we may have to endure in the meantime.

Chapter 3 - Jesus Christ is Our Saviour

The reason I need to write about Jesus Christ should be obvious, but some may not realise his importance in a proper understanding of the immortality of the soul. Therefore, I will give a brief account of his life and why he is central to every part of scripture.

The first thing I would like to clear up about Jesus Christ is his ancestry. In almost every picture, statue, or image of Jesus, he is portrayed as a tall white male with long, flowing hair. To get an accurate "picture" of Jesus, let us look at where he was born, who his mother was, and the customs he would have kept.

We have all heard the story of Jesus' birth in the city of Bethlehem to the virgin Mary, who was a Jewish woman. He was raised in the traditional Jewish ways and worshipped in their synagogues. All of his friends and his disciples were Jewish. Indeed, all the books of the bible, both old and new testaments, were written by Jews.

The average height of Jewish males at the time of Jesus was about five foot five inches, so he was not tall, and what about his long hair? We know Jesus did nothing sinful. He lived a perfect life, so he would have done nothing to dishonour Himself. This makes the following verses very interesting.

> *1Co 11:14 Doesn't even nature itself teach you that if a man has long hair, it is a dishonor to him?*

> *1Co 11:15 But if a woman has long hair, it is a glory to her, for her hair is given to her for a covering.*

Long hair on a male dishonours him, but long hair on a woman is to her glory. Therefore, Jesus would have had short hair, as was the custom of all Jewish males of his time.

As unpleasant as this will be for some people to realise. Jesus Christ was a Jew. He was born in Bethlehem but actually lived in Nazareth about ninety kilometres away. Therefore, he is sometimes referred to as Jesus the Nazarene. He was born about the year 4BC and was crucified in about 30AD. There are ongoing discussions about these dates, but for this book, they are not essential to understand.

Jesus Christ is the central figure in Christianity. The entire bible refers to Him and there are many prophecies in the old testament that point directly to Him, such as the following.

> *Isa 9:6 For to us a child is born. To us a son is given; and the government will be on his shoulders. His name will be called Wonderful, Counselor, Mighty God, Everlasting Father, Prince of Peace.*

> *Isa 9:7 Of the increase of his government and of peace there shall be no end, on David's throne, and on his kingdom, to establish it, and to uphold it with justice and with righteousness from that time on, even forever. The zeal of Yahweh of Armies will perform this.*

What has he done for us? Even his name gives us a clue to what he is. His name in the Hebrew language is Yeshua. He is also known as Christ, but this is not a part of his name. It is actually a title and not a name. The word Christ comes from the Greek word Christos and means "The Anointed One" or in Hebrew it is "Messiah".The meaning of the name Yeshua is "Jehovah Saves". That is precisely what Jesus did for us, as is clear from the following verse.

1Co 1:30 Because of him, you are in Christ Jesus, who was made to us wisdom from God, and righteousness and sanctification, and redemption:

Jesus has made us righteous, has sanctified us and redeemed us. This all simply means he has set us right with our Heavenly Father. God has accepted the sacrifice of Jesus to cover all of man's sins. We do not need to suffer because of our sins. Jesus has already paid this price for us.

1Jn 1:7 But if we walk in the light, as he is in the light, we have fellowship with one another, and the blood of Jesus Christ, his Son, cleanses us from all sin.

Those who accept Jesus Christ as their Lord of Lords and King of Kings are cleansed of all sins, not just a few or even most. We are cleaned of all sins. This is emphasised again in the following verse where he redeems us from "all iniquity" or sins.

Tit 2:14 who gave himself for us, that he might redeem us from all iniquity, and purify for himself a people for his own possession, zealous for good works.

Jesus purchased us for a price, and that price was his own death in our stead.

1Co 6:19 Or don't you know that your body is a temple of the Holy Spirit who is in you, whom you have from God? You are not your own,

1Co 6:20 for you were bought with a price. Therefore glorify God in your body and in your spirit, which are God's.

We no longer belong to ourselves. As we see in verse 20 above, we belong to God. Again reinforced in the book of 1Peter 1:18-19.

1Pe 1:18 knowing that you were redeemed, not with corruptible things, with silver or gold, from the useless way of life handed down from your fathers,

1Pe 1:19 but with precious blood, as of a lamb without blemish or spot, the blood of Christ;

Now we come to the most important part about Jesus Christ. He is the only one who can save anyone from their sins. There is no one else who can do this for us. Those who believe in other gods cannot receive eternal life, cannot put on immortality without Jesus. The following two verses make this very clear.

Act 4:12 "There is salvation in none other, for neither is there any other name under heaven, that is given among men, by which we must be saved!"

Joh 14:6 Jesus answered, "I am the way and the truth and the life. No one comes to the Father except through me."

Therefore, what we can learn from this chapter is simply this. Jesus Christ is our saviour, and the saviour of all people, or he is not a saviour for anyone. There is no room for any other possibility. It is "all or nothing".

This book was written to give you a starting point in your own studies. You are no doubt aware it is a long way from being the full story about our immortality, our future after we have reached the end of our lives, or who Jesus Christ is and what he has done for us and will continue to do for us for all eternity.

I hope you will continue to study the bible to find more answers to these and many other questions you may have about God and your relationship with Him. As you spend more time in his word, please keep the following scriptures in mind.

2Ti 3:16 All Scripture is God-breathed and is useful for teaching, rebuking, correcting and training in righteousness,

Pro 25:2 It is the glory of God to conceal a matter; to search out a matter is the glory of kings.

All scripture means both the old and the new testaments. Many people think the old testament is no longer relevant for today's Christians. Nothing could be further from the truth. So please consider yourself to be a king as you search out matters from the holy scriptures.

Along with the belief in an immortal soul are the thoughts about heaven, hell, and purgatory. It seems the way most people believe is that the good go to Heaven when they die, and the bad go to Hell. Those who go to Purgatory will eventually end up in Heaven. They need to be cleansed completely of all sins of unrighteousness before they can pass through the "Pearly Gates". I sincerely hope you can see from this chapter that the sacrifice of Jesus Christ for our sins is all we need. It will cover every sin ever committed by mankind and ever will commit.

In the following chapters, I will briefly discuss each of these topics. Then I will introduce another scenario that is not only very different from what you may believe, but one that is supported by scripture. What I have covered so far describes our souls as being mortal. The bible constantly tells us eternal life is possible for us. So now we must discuss where our futures lay and cover the three different ideas I have listed above.

The first topic will be the idea of purgatory, as a place of final cleansing before we can enter Heaven.

Chapter 4 - Purgatory, Satan's Deception

The idea of a place called purgatory is totally inconsistent with the teaching from the bible. According to Heb 10:12-14, the sacrifice of Jesus Christ on the cross made perfect those who are sanctified. Surely this means they are right with God and can enter his Kingdom, with no need to be purified beforehand. Christ's sacrifice has made them perfect.

Heb 10:12 but he, when he had offered one sacrifice for sins forever, sat down on the right hand of God;

Heb 10:13 from that time waiting until his enemies are made the footstool of his feet.

Heb 10:14 For by one offering he has perfected forever those who are being sanctified.

Perfected for ever, surely this means without sin, and if this is the case, then there is no need for a place to be scourged of remaining sins before entering Heaven. Consider what is recorded for us in Gal 2:16.

Gal 2:16 yet knowing that a man is not justified by the works of the law but through faith in Jesus Christ, even we believed in Christ Jesus, that we might be justified by faith in Christ, and not by the works of the law, because no flesh will be justified by the works of the law.

This verse makes it very clear how we are justified before God. It is by our own faith in Jesus Christ as our Lord of Lords and King of Kings. Nothing to do with any type of works. Not our own, or the works of others on our behalf, when we are supposedly in Purgatory waiting to be scourged of the remaining sins that the blood of Jesus Christ was not good enough to cleanse us from.

The bible tells us in many places that when Jesus died for all mankind on the cross, this sacrifice was sufficient. Read Rom 5:18-21 to see the same idea explained again.

> *Rom 5:18 So then as through one trespass, all men were condemned; even so through one act of righteousness, all men were justified to life.*

> *Rom 5:19 For as through the one man's disobedience many were made sinners, even so through the obedience of the one, many will be made righteous.*

> *Rom 5:20 The law came in besides, that the trespass might abound; but where sin abounded, grace abounded more exceedingly;*

> *Rom 5:21 that as sin reigned in death, even so grace might reign through righteousness to eternal life through Jesus Christ our Lord.*

When we are united with Christ, we are totally cleansed of all sins. Our sins were nailed to the cross, as explained in the following verses.

> *Col 2:12 having been buried with him in baptism, in which you were also raised with him through faith in the working of God, who raised him from the dead.*

> *Col 2:13 You were dead through your trespasses and the uncircumcision of your flesh. He made you alive together with him, having forgiven us all our trespasses,*

> *Col 2:14 wiping out the handwriting in ordinances which was against us; and he has taken it out of the way, nailing it to the cross;*

Jesus Christ has taken our sins on Himself and has dealt with them on our behalf. How can we possibly be in Jesus, but still sinful? It makes little sense to believe this. More proof follows.

> *2Co 5:21 For him who knew no sin he made to be sin on our behalf; so that in him we might become the righteousness of God.*

> *Rom 6:23 For the wages of sin is death, but the free gift of God is eternal life in Christ Jesus our Lord.*

So, from these few verses above, we learn several things. First Hebrews 10:14 tells us we are perfected forever. Second, in Romans 5:21, righteousness will reign through Jesus Christ. Third, in Colossians 2:13, all our trespasses are forgiven. They have been nailed to the cross. Fourth, in 2 Corinthians 5:21 we become the righteousness of God and then in Romans 6:23 we see where we can have the free gift of God that is eternal life in Jesus Christ.

The last scripture I will use here is powerful. That should have you believe we are completely clean of all sins and unrighteousness thanks to what Jesus did for us by his self sacrifice on the cross.

> *1Jn 1:7 But if we walk in the light, as he is in the light, we have fellowship with one another, and the blood of Jesus Christ, his Son, cleanses us from all sin.*

To believe in purgatory is to believe the death and resurrection of Jesus Christ is not enough to take away our sins. When he died on the cross, he only did a part of the job of saving us from our sins and now we must add to his work of salvation. We must do more. We must be scourged to make us clean. This is completely against the clear teachings of the bible. Another part of this purgatory idea is your relatives, who are still alive, can pay "indulgences" to the church to help you get out of purgatory and into Heaven sooner.

The idea of purgatory is not a biblical one. I sincerely hope you can see this from the above scriptures. Please ask yourself these questions.

Does the sacrifice of Jesus Christ cover our sins or not? (1Jo 1:7)

Does God give us eternal life as a free gift? (Rom 6:23)

Does the sacrifice of Jesus Christ make those who are being sanctified perfect? (Heb 10:14)

When Jesus Christ offered Himself as a sacrifice, was it one sacrifice to cover all sins forever? (Heb 10:12)

Is it from our faith in Jesus Christ that we are saved? (2Co 2:12)

If you can answer "yes" to any of these questions, then how do you conclude that when Jesus Christ died for all people on the cross, he only did half of the job of cleansing us of our sins? Why do we need to add to the sanctifying work of our Lord?

What does the word of God have to say about being justified by doing anything other than hearing and believing the truth?

> *Rom 3:28 We maintain therefore that a man is justified by faith apart from the works of the law.*
>
> *Gal 3:2 I just want to learn this from you: Did you receive the Spirit by the works of the law, or by hearing of faith?*
>
> *Act 13:39 and by him everyone who believes is justified from all things, from which you could not be justified by the law of Moses.*
>
> *Gal 2:16 yet knowing that a man is not justified by the works of the law but through faith in Jesus Christ, even we believed in Christ Jesus, that we might be justified by faith in Christ, and*

not by the works of the law, because no flesh will be justified by the works of the law.

What have we seen from the above verses? Justification is by faith in Jesus Christ. We can never be justified by keeping the law, not that we do not need to keep the law, we need to keep it. But our justification is only by faith. If you have this true faith in Jesus, then you will automatically want to keep the law. As you come to know Jesus, you will also come to know the benefits of keeping his laws. In the book of Matthew 22:37-40, Jesus gives us the two greatest commandments, and they are to love God and to love your fellow man. If we all lived this way, there would be no more crime or poverty in the world.

We are only saved by believing in Jesus, as the following passage of scripture makes it very plain for those who will listen to the words of God, and actually believe them.

Rom 10:9 that if you will confess with your mouth that Jesus is Lord, and believe in your heart that God raised him from the dead, you will be saved.

Rom 10:10 For with the heart, one believes unto righteousness; and with the mouth confession is made unto salvation.

Rom 10:11 For the Scripture says, "Whoever believes in him will not be disappointed."

Rom 10:12 For there is no distinction between Jew and Greek; for the same Lord is Lord of all, and is rich to all who call on him.

Rom 10:13 For, "Whoever will call on the name of the Lord will be saved."

Rom 10:14 How then will they call on him in whom they have not believed? How will they believe in him whom they have not heard? How will they hear without a preacher?

Rom 10:15 And how will they preach unless they are sent? As it is written: "How beautiful are the feet of those who preach the Good News of peace, who bring glad tidings of good things!"

Rom 10:16 But they didn't all listen to the glad news. For Isaiah says, "Lord, who has believed our report?"

Rom 10:17 So faith comes by hearing, and hearing by the word of God.

Some People who believe in this fictional place called purgatory say it is a good thing, and has a real purpose in cleansing us from our sins. But surely the best thing possible is to be thoroughly cleansed from all sins just by believing in Jesus Christ, and his self sacrifice for all mankind. If Jesus has done this for us, then there is absolutely no need for a place where our sins are further scourged from us. By the actions of Jesus, and our faith in Him, there is no trace of any sin left in us. Therefore, we are at peace with God, and we should also be at peace with ourselves.

Why Does It Matter?

Believing in a place called Purgatory, is to believe the sacrifice of Jesus Christ on the cross only partially cleansed us from our sins. But this is contrary to what we read earlier in the last chapter in.

1Jn 1:7 But if we walk in the light, as he is in the light, we have fellowship with one another, and the blood of Jesus Christ, his Son, cleanses us from all sin.

Christ's death on the cross cleanses us from ALL sin. Therefore there is absolutely no need for a place where we undergo further cleansing. This is a false teaching, no doubt having it's origins in the "Father of Lies", or Satan.

Chapter 5 - The Truth About Hell

The idea of hell as a place of eternal punishing for those who do evil has been used for centuries to keep sinners in line. The old-fashioned "fire and brimstone" style of preaching was very effective when preaching to the illiterate. They have no way of exploring the word of God for themselves, so they believe what they are told. This form of preaching should be of little use today, as most people are no longer illiterate. The vast majority of Christians have their own bibles to read.

The only problem now, is that people still do not read or study their bible to find the truth. They are still content to accept what they are told. But if you are seeking the truth about this place called hell, then the bible must be your only source of knowledge. With that thought in mind, let us explore this topic.

God Is Omnipresent.

Christians must believe in the omnipresence of God. This means that there is no place in all of creation that God is not present. He created the entire universe, so he can obviously be present in any part of his creation. So let us see where God must be. We understand he dwells In Heaven; he is present there. He is also present here on the earth, even though we cannot see Him. And now what about this place called hell? If it is a part of his creation, then he must be present there as well. I know this will cause many arguments, but either God is omnipresent, or he is not omnipresent. He cannot be both.

So what does God see when he is in Hell? It is his children created in his image, whom he loves, and they are being tormented by the fires of hell for all eternity.

God is love, and his love for everyone is the same. It is total, complete, and it is unconditional. Unlike most humans, who only love people if it suits them. So everyone in this place called Hell is loved by God, and God will watch them suffer for all eternity. This concept is one I struggled with in my early teenage years, even before I looked into God's holy scriptures for any answers to this dilemma.

So what does the bible say on the matter of eternal punishing in Hell? The answer to that can be found in Rom 6:23.

> *Rom 6:23 For the wages of sin is death, but the free gift of God is eternal life in Christ Jesus our Lord.*

This verse reveals the truth for anyone who will believe God's words over the teaching of men. It exposes two very different and opposing ideas. And they are death and life. Two diametrically opposite ideas.

Do you understand the start of this verse? The wages of sin are death. Not everlasting punishing, but death, and death is the exact opposite to life. If you are paid the correct wages for the sins you have committed according to this verse, those wages are death. You will no longer be alive, and if this is the case, then how can your punishing be eternal?

Life eternal is a gift from God, as we see in the last part of this verse. A loving God would never subject even those who sin against Him to this type of punishment.

If hell is a place of eternal punishing, then consider the fate of an atheist who has lived a good life apart from his unbelief in God. He has volunteered to help the needy. And has shown compassion for those less fortunate than himself. He may have lived the type of life God wants us to live, except he cannot believe in God. Is this man now going to suffer in hell for all of eternity for this? We must remember the character of God. He is loving, compassionate, slow to anger and forgiving. I simply cannot comprehend a God being so harsh as to commit this man to be punished for all time without end.

Please do not misunderstand me here. I definitely believe in a place called hell, and the wicked will end up there. But it is a totally different outcome for sinners than what most Christians believe today.

It is unfortunate that the idea of an immortal soul also means the souls of the wicked must go somewhere after the body dies. And of course, this would be correct, but only if the soul is immortal. What if the soul was not immortal and could be annihilated completely? If the soul could be subjected to eternal destruction, then the idea of going to either Heaven or Hell for all eternity is now debatable.

Let me repeat Rom 6:23 here as a reminder of the wages of sin.

> *Rom 6:23 For the wages of sin is death, but the free gift of God is eternal life in Christ Jesus our Lord.*

The wages of sin are death. Now with this thought in mind, please read Mat 10:28 from the new testament, and then Eze 18:4 from the old testament to reinforce my comments earlier.

> *Mat 10:28 Don't be afraid of those who kill the body, but are not able to kill the soul. Rather, fear him who is able to destroy both soul and body in Gehenna.*

> *Eze 18:4 Behold, all souls are mine; as the soul of the father, so also the soul of the son is mine. The soul who sins, he shall die.*

Notice what these verses are saying about the soul that sins. It can be killed. Therefore, souls can die, and from Mat 10:28, we can plainly see that God has the power to destroy both the body and the soul in Gehenna, or hell. Again, the immortality of the soul is proven to be a false understanding.

This thought makes the meaning of Mal 4:3 in the old testament very clear.

Mal 4:3 "You shall tread down the wicked; for they will be ashes under the soles of your feet in the day that I make," says Yahweh of Armies.

The wicked will be ashes under the feet of the righteous. They will be destroyed by God in the fires of Gehenna, the fires of hell. This is the reward for the wicked. Complete and permanent destruction in the fires of hell. Not suffering in these fires for all time. No, just total destruction. Ashes to ashes, dust to dust. The actions of a loving God.

The best known and most repeated scripture in the entire bible must be Joh 3:16 recorded below.

Joh 3:16 For God so loved the world, that he gave his one and only Son, that whoever believes in him should not perish, but have eternal life.

Check out Deu 30:19 below to see further proof of the soul that sins will die.

Deu 30:19 I call heaven and earth to witness against you today, that I have set before you life and death, the blessing and the curse. Therefore choose life, that you may live, you and your descendants;

We are here given two options. Choose either life or death. Death here does not mean eternal life suffering in hell. No, it means exactly what it is saying. Death, a cessation from life. So what can we learn from all we have read so far? It is he who believes in Jesus has eternal life. Therefore, those who do not believe in Jesus do not have eternal life. There is no other alternative. Either life or death.

Mortal Sin.

Is there any sin that cannot be forgiven by God? Only those who blaspheme against the Holy Spirit will not be forgiven. Otherwise, the answer to that question is simply no. God can forgive any sin that we confess and repent of. This includes the worst sins you can imagine. Verse two below tells us to confess our sins and he (Jesus) will forgive us and cleanse us from all unrighteousness.

> *1Jn 1:8 If we say that we have no sin, we deceive ourselves, and the truth is not in us.*

> *1Jn 1:9 If we confess our sins, he is faithful and righteous to forgive us the sins, and to cleanse us from all unrighteousness.*

> *1Jn 1:10 If we say that we haven't sinned, we make him a liar, and his word is not in us.*

It is assumed by many traditional churches today that anyone who commits a mortal sin is cut off from the sanctifying grace of God. This deceives people and heaps shame onto them and will drive them away from Jesus instead of drawing them to Him.

We are all sinners. Some sins are committed before being called to Jesus and others after having been called. These sins may temporarily interrupt your relationship with God, but they will never separate you from his grace. The only sin that can be mortal is the one we refuse to repent of. If someone sins and then seeks God's forgiveness, they will once again be set right with God. But the repentance must be genuine. You cannot fool God with a phoney repentance.

> *Rom 3:21 But now apart from the law, a righteousness of God has been revealed, being testified by the law and the prophets;*

Rom 3:22 even the righteousness of God through faith in Jesus Christ to all and on all those who believe. For there is no distinction,

Rom 3:23 for all have sinned, and fall short of the glory of God;

Rom 3:24 being justified freely by his grace through the redemption that is in Christ Jesus;

Rom 3:25 whom God sent to be an atoning sacrifice, through faith in his blood, for a demonstration of his righteousness through the passing over of prior sins, in God's forbearance;

Rom 3:26 to demonstrate his righteousness at this present time; that he might himself be just, and the justifier of him who has faith in Jesus.

That is an amazing piece of scripture. Thanks to the sacrifice of our Lord on the cross, we are justified if we repent and confess our sins to God. Having faith in Jesus is the only way to receive forgiveness, salvation and eternal life.

Chapter 6 - Do We Go To Heaven When We Die?

Now I will discuss the idea of the good going to Heaven when they die. I believe this to be just another false teaching. Now if you consider all the wonderful people from the old testament, you have to ask if any of them ascended into Heaven. The answer is found in John 3:13 below.

Joh3:13 No one has ascended into heaven, but he who descended out of heaven, the Son of Man, who is in heaven.

Here is another question, When the bible here says that no one has ascended in to heaven, does it mean no one? Surely it does, so let us just accept the word of God to mean what it says.

Next, let us look at Hebrews chapter 11. The people mentioned here were all praised for their faith. Some big names are here, including Noah, Abraham, Sarah, Isaac, and Jacob, to name a few. Then, at the end of this chapter, we read the following two verses.

Heb 11:39 These all, having had testimony given to them through their faith, didn't receive the promise,

Heb 11:40 God having provided some better thing concerning us, so that apart from us they should not be made perfect.

None of these amazing people received their rewards. None of these mighty men and women of God have entered their ultimate reward. The reason is in the last verse. They will be made perfect when Jesus returns in all power and glory. Meanwhile, they sleep, awaiting their resurrection from the dead. Rev 20:5 tells us the first resurrection of the dead will only occur after Jesus has returned, and Satan has been bound and cast into the abyss.

Jesus Christ has not returned yet, therefore, no one has ascended into heaven. It isn't the right time for Jesus to return. It is clear from verse 40 below that the dead will be raised from their sleep when Jesus Christ returns.

> *Joh 6:39 This is the will of my Father who sent me, that of all he has given to me I should lose nothing, but should raise him up at the last day.*

> *Joh 6:40 This is the will of the one who sent me, that everyone who sees the Son, and believes in him, should have eternal life; and I will raise him up at the last day.*

When Christ made the statement "This is the will of the one who sent me, that everyone who sees the Son, and believes in him, should have eternal life; and I will raise him up at the last day, sums up a cornerstone of Christian faith. It speaks to the core of salvation, faith, and the promise of eternal life through belief in Jesus Christ.

This statement outlines a fundamental doctrine of Christianity—the path to eternal life lies in recognizing Jesus Christ as the Son of God and placing faith in him. It emphasizes the divine will, revealing that God desires all individuals to experience eternal life through a personal relationship with Christ.

The act of "seeing the Son" goes beyond mere visual awareness, it signifies understanding, acknowledging, and embracing the teachings, life, and divinity of Jesus Christ. Belief, in this context, covers more than intellectual acknowledgement; it involves a deep and thorough trust and acceptance of Jesus as the source of salvation and eternal life.

Furthermore, the promise of being raised up at the last day offers assurance and hope. It affirms that those who have faith in Christ will experience a resurrection from the dead at the completion of the age.

This verse sums up the essence of Christian faith, a call to recognize Christ's divinity, believe in him for eternal life, and trust in the promise of the resurrection. It serves as a beacon of hope, offering solace and assurance of a incomparable existence beyond our earthly life for all who embrace the Son of God and his teachings.

In the old testament, death is described as sleeping. Read the book of 1Kings in the old testament and especially from chapter eleven. When anyone died, they were said to have "slept with their fathers". Death is likened to sleep because it is only temporary, even though some have been asleep for thousands of years. The dead are waiting for the resurrection.

Now I would like to close this chapter with the following verses from Rev 22:12-14.

> *Rev 22:12 Behold, I come quickly. My reward is with me, to repay to each man according to his work.*

This statement from Jesus Christ encapsulates the promise of Christ's imminent return and the principle of divine judgment based on one's actions.

The phrase "I come quickly" speaks to the anticipation of Christ's second coming, emphasizing the imminence and suddenness of His arrival. It serves as a reminder to be prepared and vigilant, as this event will unfold unexpectedly.

Moreover, the assurance that "My reward is with me" underscores the concept of divine justice. It signifies that Christ, upon His return, will bring rewards or consequences in accordance with each individual's deeds. This idea of divine recompense highlights the significance of personal actions and the accountability that accompanies them in the grand scheme of salvation.

The phrase "to repay to each man according to his work", emphasizes the principle of judgment based on one's actions. It reinforces the belief that salvation is not merely a result of faith but also intertwined with the manner of life one leads, the choices made, and the impact of those actions on others.

This declaration serves as a call to live a life of righteousness and purpose, understanding that our actions have consequences and will be evaluated in the divine judgment. It instils a sense of responsibility and encourages a life guided by moral principles and compassion, with the awareness that our deeds will ultimately shape our eternal destiny.

This is followed by Jesus making the famous and well known statement in Rev 22:13.

> *Rev 22:13 I am the Alpha and the Omega, the First and the Last, the Beginning and the End.*

"I am the Alpha and the Omega, the First and the Last, the Beginning and the End" is a potent declaration by Jesus Christ himself. This powerful statement summarizes the divine nature, eternal existence, and omnipotence of Christ.

The title "Alpha and Omega" refers to the first and last letters of the Greek alphabet, symbolizing completeness and totality. By claiming this title, Christ asserts His role as the beginning and the end of all things, signifying His eternal nature and sovereignty over the entirety of existence. This declaration encompasses the concept of divine omnipresence, enveloping all time and space.

"I am the Alpha and the Omega" serves as a profound affirmation of Christ's divinity, His eternal nature, and His central role in the grand narrative of existence. It transcends the boundaries of time, affirming His presence in the past, present, and future, offering assurance and comfort to those who place their faith in His eternal being.

Moreover, by identifying as the "First and the Last," Christ affirms His pre-eminence and supremacy over all creation. This title establishes His authority, indicating that before anything existed, He was present, and after everything passes, He will endure.

Furthermore, as the "Beginning and the End," Christ embodies the entirety of existence itself. This proclamation signifies that He is the source from which all things originate and the ultimate culmination and fulfilment of all creation's purpose. This verse is followed by Rev 22:14.

> *Rev 22:14 Blessed are those who do his commandments, that they may have the right to the tree of life, and may enter in by the gates into the city.*

The phrase "Blessed are those who do his commandments, that they may have the right to the tree of life, and may enter in by the gates into the city" presents a powerful message about the significance of obedience, blessings, and access to eternal life.

This verse echoes a consistent theme throughout the bible; the value of following divine directives. It emphasizes that those who adhere to God's commandments are blessed and granted a special privilege: the right to partake in the tree of life. The tree of life symbolizes immortality, eternal life, and divine favour, signifying a spiritual reward for obedience and fidelity.

Moreover, it introduces the imagery of entering the city through its gates. This imagery signifies access to a sacred and heavenly realm. It represents a realm of peace, fulfilment, and divine presence reserved for those who align their lives with the will of God.

The phrase encapsulates the idea that obedience isn't merely a set of rules, but a pathway to spiritual fulfilment and the ultimate reward of eternal life. It speaks to the deep spiritual connection between adhering to divine principles, and reaping the blessings and privileges associated with a life lived in alignment with the principles of God.

In essence, "Blessed are those who do his commandments" emphasizes the profound link between obedience, blessings, and access to eternal life. It serves as a reminder of the spiritual significance of following divine guidance and the promise of a transcendent existence for those who walk the path of righteousness.

I hope you can understand what is revealed here, because it tells us several things. First, Jesus is returning soon and what is he bringing with Him? It is his reward. And just what is this reward? Our answer is in verse 14. The tree of life is theirs. The tree Adam and Eve should have eaten from and received eternal life. Then the last part of verse 14 is a clue that leads us into the next chapter. They may enter by the gates into the city. Notice it is not into Heaven, but into the city. What city is this?

Chapter 7 - The New Heavens, Earth, and Jerusalem

The final destination for those who have faith in Jesus Christ, and have their names written in the book of life, will be the New Jerusalem that will come down out of Heaven. But there is a great deal to happen prior to that event. Jesus Christ will return to this earth and rule over all nations in great power and glory. This is recorded for us in the following passage of scripture from the book of Revelation.

> *Rev 20:1 Then I saw an angel descending from heaven, having the key of the abyss, and a great chain in his hand.*
>
> *Rev 20:2 And he took hold of the dragon, the ancient serpent, who is the Devil and Satan, and bound him for a thousand years.*
>
> *Rev 20:3 Then he cast him into the abyss, and locked him up, and sealed the abyss over him, so that he would not deceive the nations any longer until the thousand years were fulfilled; and after that it is ordained that he be loosed for a short time.*
>
> *Rev 20:4 And I saw thrones; and they that sat upon them, and judgment was given to them; and I saw the souls of those who had been beheaded for the testimony of Jesus, and for the Word of God, and those who did not worship the beast, or his image, and did not receive the mark in their foreheads or in their hands; and they lived and reigned with Christ a thousand years.*

The vivid imagery of an angel descending from heaven, wielding the key of the abyss and holding a great chain in his hand. This symbolic vision embodies profound spiritual concepts, representing divine authority, judgment, and the ultimate triumph of good over evil.

The angel's descent from heaven signifies a celestial origin and divine sanction, emphasizing the authority vested in this celestial being. Holding the key of the abyss symbolizes control and dominion over dark, evil and spiritual forces. The abyss represents a realm of spiritual confinement, often associated with evil or chaotic entities, and the possession of the key indicates power over those cast into the pit.

Chains are symbols of captivity or confinement, indicating the angel's ability to contain or control the forces that might bring harm or chaos.

This powerful imagery signifies a moment of divine intervention, where celestial forces act to bring order, restrain evil, and uphold divine justice. It speaks to the overarching theme of spiritual warfare, depicting the eventual triumph of righteousness over darkness.

In a broader sense, this vision inspires hope, reminding believers that ultimately, the power of good will prevail. It instils confidence in the divine plan, reinforcing the belief in a higher authority that ensures the containment and defeat of the evil spiritual forces, paving the way for a future where goodness and light triumph.

Therefore, when Jesus returns, it will be to rule over this earth for 1,000 years. When he does return, this world will be in an unbelievably horrific mess. The 24th chapter of the book of Matthew describes events that will occur prior to Christ's return. This describes a world at war. Compare this with the book of Revelation, a book very few ministers of religion will preach about, and you will get an idea as to the extent of the devastation on this world before Jesus returns.

It is only after this 1,000 years of Jesus ruling the world that we will see the city that the previous chapter was referring to, "The New Jerusalem". This is the final dwelling place for Christ's followers. Not in Heaven, or on a cloud somewhere thumbing away on a harp for all of eternity. No, our future dwelling place is none other than "The New Jerusalem". God has revealed this in his written word in Rev 21:1-4.

> *Rev 21:1 I saw a new heaven and a new earth: for the first heaven and the first earth have passed away, and the sea is no more.*

> *Rev 21:2 I saw the holy city, New Jerusalem, coming down out of heaven from God, prepared like a bride adorned for her husband.*

> *Rev 21:3 I heard a loud voice out of heaven saying, "Behold, God's dwelling is with people, and he will dwell with them, and they will be his people, and God himself will be with them as their God. "*

> *Rev 21:4 He will wipe away every tear from their eyes. Death will be no more; neither will there be mourning, nor crying, nor pain, any more. The first things have passed away.*

> *The new Heaven, the new earth, and the new Jerusalem. The first earth, where we are now living, will pass away and there will be no more sea. God will live with his people in the Holy City, which will come down from Heaven. And as we have seen in this book so far, those who are God's people are only those who believe in Jesus Christ as their Lord of Lords and Kings of Kings. Only those who have had their names entered into "The book of life".*

If this new Jerusalem comes down from Heaven, then obviously it is not in heaven, and therefore if we are to inhabit this new city, then we will not be in Heaven either. This is where the righteous will spend eternity, as is made clear in Rev 3:11-12.

Rev 3:11 I am coming quickly! Hold firmly that which you have, so that no one takes your crown.

Rev 3:12 He who overcomes, I will make him a pillar in the temple of my God, and he will go out from there no more. I will write on him the name of my God, and the name of the city of my God, the new Jerusalem, which comes down out of heaven from my God, and my own new name.

He who overcomes is the one who remains faithful to Jesus Christ and who dwells in this new Jerusalem. He is also the one who will inherit immortality. These new Heavens and new Earth are also mentioned in a prophesy from the old testament in Isaiah 65:17-25.

Isa 65:17 For, behold, I create new heavens and a new earth; and the former things will not be remembered, nor come into mind.

Isa 65:18 But be glad and rejoice forever in that which I create; for, behold, I create Jerusalem to be a delight, and her people a joy.

Isa 65:19 I will rejoice in Jerusalem, and delight in my people; and the voice of weeping and the voice of crying will be heard in her no more.

Isa 65:20 No more will there be an infant who only lives a few days, nor an old man who has not filled his days; for the child will die one hundred years old, and the sinner being one hundred years old will be accursed.

Isa 65:21 They will build houses, and inhabit them. They will plant vineyards, and eat their fruit.

Isa 65:22 They will not build, and another inhabit. They will not plant, and another eat: for the days of my people will be like the days of a tree, and my chosen will long enjoy the work of their hands.

Isa 65:23 They will not labor in vain, nor give birth for calamity; for they are the offspring of Yahweh's blessed, and their descendants with them.

Isa 65:24 It will happen that, before they call, I will answer; and while they are yet speaking, I will hear.

Isa 65:25 The wolf and the lamb will feed together, and the lion will eat straw like the ox. Dust will be the serpent's food. They will not hurt nor destroy in all my holy mountain, says Yahweh.

You can see from these passages of scripture, from the old testament, that the idea of new heavens and new earth is not a recent, or new testament idea only. It has been on God's "drawing board" for thousands of years. All of God's prophesies are certain to eventuate. Many of them have already come to pass with many more still in the future. But the word of God is sure and his promises are certain to be fulfilled at their proper time.

The thought of a "New Jerusalem" is reinforced in the following scriptures.

Rev 21:1, I saw a new heaven and a new earth: for the first heaven and the first earth have passed away, and the sea is no more.

Now that we have a new Heaven and earth, what follows next, we see this is the next verse from Rev 21:2-5

Rev 21:2 I saw the holy city, New Jerusalem, coming down out of heaven from God, prepared like a bride adorned for her husband.

Rev 21:3 I heard a loud voice out of heaven saying, "Behold, God's dwelling is with people, and he will dwell with them, and they will be his people, and God himself will be with them as their God.

Rev 21:4 He will wipe away every tear from their eyes. Death will be no more; neither will there be mourning, nor crying, nor pain, any more. The first things have passed away."

Rev 21:5 He who sits on the throne said, "Behold, I am making all things new." He said, "Write, for these words of God are faithful and true."

Just a few things are worth noting about this "New Jerusalem" from the 21st chapter of Revelation.

1. It will be a holy city.

2. God will also dwell in this city.

3. There will be no need for a temple. God and Jesus will be the temple.

4. No need for the sun or the moon because God will be its light.

5. The gates will never be closed.

6. But only those whose names are in the book of life may enter.

7. This city will come down out of Heaven.

8. God will wipe away every tear from our eyes.

9. There will be no more death, dying, sorrow, or pain.

10. God will make everything new.

If you read through this chapter, you will find more ways God will reward those who love Him. There is no way we mere mortal humans can know what the future holds. Look at what God tells us in 1Co 2:9.

> *1Co 2:9 But as it is written, "Things which an eye didn't see, and an ear didn't hear, which didn't enter into the heart of man, these God has prepared for those who love him."*

We do not know the exact time for this new earth, new heavens, and new Jerusalem. But since it is one of God's promises to us, it is going to happen sometime in the future. And that time will be according to God's own timetable, not ours. But we know that only those whose names are written in the Lamb's book of life will enjoy this new creation.

And as we see in 2Pe 3:10-13 below, we are told how we should live our lives today, if we want to inhabit this amazing new city from God.

> *2Pe 3:10 But the day of the Lord will come as a thief in the night; in which the heavens will pass away with a great noise, and the elements will be dissolved with fervent heat, and the earth and the works that are in it will be burned up.*

> *2Pe 3:11 Therefore since all these things will be destroyed like this, what kind of people ought you to be in holy living and godliness,*

> *2Pe 3:12 looking for and earnestly desiring the coming of the day of God, which will cause the burning heavens to be dissolved, and the elements will melt with fervent heat?*

> *2Pe 3:13 But, according to his promise, we look for new heavens and a new earth, in which righteousness dwells.*

We must all go before the Judgement seat at the Great White Throne judgement.

> *Rev 20:11 I saw a great white throne, and him who sat on it, from whose face the earth and the heaven fled away. There was found no place for them.*

> *Rev 20:12 I saw the dead, the great and the small, standing before the throne, and they opened books. Another book was opened, which is the book of life. The dead were judged out of the things which were written in the books, according to their works.*

> *Rev 20:13 The sea gave up the dead who were in it. Death and Hades gave up the dead who were in them. They were judged, each one according to his works.*

> *Rev 20:14 Death and Hades were thrown into the lake of fire. This is the second death, the lake of fire.*

> *Rev 20:15 If anyone was not found written in the book of life, he was cast into the lake of fire.*

Verse 15 is very clear. Anyone whose name is not in the book of life will be cast into the lake of fire. And as I wrote earlier, this will be the second death from which there will be no returning, ashes to ashes and dust to dust is the ultimate fate for these people who refuse to accept Jesus Christ as their Lord of Lords and King of Kings.

This book was written to discuss the "immortality of the soul", and this is where it is all leading to. If your name is in the Lamb's book of life, you will have an immortal soul and will dwell in the incredible new Jerusalem. You will continue to exist in perfect peace, health, safety, and comfort. You will live with Jesus Christ and God the Father. There will be no more death, sorrow, pain, or suffering. The future is indeed a glorious one.

But if your name is not in that all important book, your future is very short as you are cast into the lake of fire to be completely consumed by its flames.

The choice where you will end up is totally in your own hands. God will never force you to do anything you do not want to do. Therefore, I will leave you here with some more sound advice from God's own words, as recorded in Deu 30:19.

> *Deu 30:19 I call heaven and earth to witness against you today, that I have set before you life and death, the blessing and the curse. Therefore choose life, that you may live, you and your descendants;*

Chapter 8 - Conclusion

I understand that what I have said in this book will be very different from what you may already believe. I have attempted to backup everything I have said from the word of God. His holy bible. All I ask is that you will read with an open mind. Examine the scriptures I have quoted from, and judge for yourself if I am right or wrong.

But be forewarned. If you decide I am correct, you may receive a great deal of resistance from your family and friends who may not agree with you. Changing how you view the mortality of the soul, should make you want to live a life seeking what you do not have. Immortality.

This immortality can only be gained by having faith in our Lord and Saviour Jesus Christ. You must accept him as the only authority over your life. Remember what God the Father said on the day Jesus was baptised in the river by John the Baptist as recorded in

Mat 17:5 While he was still speaking, behold, a bright cloud overshadowed them. Behold, a voice came out of the cloud, saying, "This is my beloved Son, in whom I am well pleased. Listen to him."

Also remember what the Prophet Moses wrote in

Deu 18:15 Yahweh your God will raise up to you a prophet from among you, of your brothers, like me. You shall listen to him.

Moses is regarded as the greatest prophet from the old testament. Here he is talking about one greater than himself, and that can only be Jesus Christ. Both he and our Heavenly Father have both given us the instructions to "listen to him". Listen to Jesus Christ.

Thank you for reading this book, and may our gracious Lord bless you and your family.

About The Author

Leslie Rendell worked most of his life in an agricultural support industry, mostly in the supply of spare parts for machinery. Since his retirement in 2014 he has dedicated much of his time to bible study and writing books as he comes to understand biblical topics.

He understands the bible is a very complex book and one that is easy to misinterpret and believes this is one of the main reasons why there are so many different version of the bible and different religions around the world.

What he writes is his own interpretation of God's holy scriptures. He studies the thoughts of other writers to try to see things from their point of view, but always comes back to the bible as the final authority on any topic. His main aim in writing, is to give anyone who is seeking the truth from God's words a starting point in their own research.

Leslie's other interest are photography, and his growing family.

Don't miss out!

Visit the website below and you can sign up to receive emails whenever Leslie Rendell publishes a new book. There's no charge and no obligation.

https://books2read.com/r/B-A-VDUV-JXTEC

BOOKS 2 READ

Connecting independent readers to independent writers.

Also by Leslie Rendell

Bible Studies
Three Days and Three Nights
According To Your Faith
Do Not Conform
How Long Was Jesus Christ in the Tomb
The Law of Moses
Abraham, Jesus and the Cross
Do We Have Immortal Souls
Be Holy
Is Being Fearful A Sin Against God
Mockers and the Return of Jesus Christ
Teachers During The Tribulation
Tearing of The Curtain in The Temple
The Thief On The Cross Alongside Jesus Christ
What Is The Rapture
The Imminence of the Rapture is a False Teaching.
Why The Pre-Tribulation Rapture Theory Is False
Are You Hindered By Satan
Satan is Targeting Man's Free Will
Why Is There So Much Suffering In Our World
The Sign of Jonah
Evil Is The Rejection Of God
Satan, Spirit Being With Many Names

Have Faith In God
Only One Sign
The Lord's Passover
The Resurrection of Jesus Christ

Watch for more at https://www.leslierendell.com.

About the Author

Leslie Rendell has been studying the bible for most of his life. When he is researching a topic, he looks at what other people have said in their books, or on the world wide web. He believes it is important to see opinions from every angle of a subject to be able to give his own informed decision. But still the most important reference is always the bible. There is no other authority when it comes to matters of what God expects from those He has created in His own image. If there is a conflict between the bible and man's thoughts, The bible will win every time. All though he has not had any formal bible education, he believes the bible can be understood by the average bible reader. Otherwise how could they ever understand what God's will is for their lives? Apart from bible studies, Leslie loves to spend time with his family watching his daughter grow into a wonderful woman and mother. His grand children starting on their life journeys, and now some great grand children to watch growing up. It is a special time in his life to see his family grow. He is retired and now lives in the South West of Western Australia. Apart from his love of the Bible and his family, his other hobby is photography, where he loves to photograph God's creation.